Step-by-Step
Collage

Judy Balchin

Search Press

First published in Great Britain 2002

Search Press Limited
Wellwood, North Farm Road,
Tunbridge Wells, Kent TN2 3DR

Reprinted 2004, 2005, 2010

Text copyright © Judy Balchin 2002

Photographs by Charlotte de la Bédoyère,
Search Press Studios
Photographs and design copyright © Search Press Ltd 2002

ISBN 978 1 903975 34 3

Suppliers
If you have difficulty in obtaining any of the materials and equipment mentioned in this book, then please visit the Search Press website for details of suppliers: www.searchpress.com

Alternatively, you can write to the Publishers at the address above, for a current list of stockists, which includes firms who operate a mail-order service.

Acknowledgements
The Publishers have been unable to trace the copyright holder of the paper collage 'Tree of Life' by H. Roger Rodgers, supplied by Bridgeman Art Library, on page 5. We would be grateful to receive any information as to their identity.

Printed in China by WKT Company Ltd

To my creative niece, Briony

A big thank you to the creative and hard-working team at Search Press for their energy and enthusiasm.

The Publishers would like to say a huge thank you to Mushed Miah, Mofe Jones Odeh, Ben Kersey, Christopher Armour, Ellie Hayward, Charlie de la Bédoyère, Jacklyn Kwan, Arlo Holman, Sarah Lusack, Isaac Holman and Jessika Kwan.

Finally, special thanks to Southborough Primary School, Tunbridge Wells.

When this sign is used in the book, it means that adult supervision is needed.

REMEMBER!
Ask an adult to help you when you see this sign.

Contents

Introduction 4

Materials 6

Sea Scene 8

Butterflies 10

Roman Mosaic 12

Creepy Crawlies 14

Sunflower Card 16

Fairy Card 18

Junk Truck 20

Egyptian God 22

Leaf Card 24

Alien 26

Techniques 28

Patterns 29

Index 32

Introduction

You have probably been creating collages for years without even knowing it. The word 'collage' comes from the French word meaning 'to stick' and we can all remember creating pictures by sticking paper shapes on to a piece of card.

Over the years, many artists have used collage in their work. Matisse was a very famous French artist. As he got older, he found painting quite difficult, so he started tearing and cutting up pieces of coloured paper to make his pictures.

Beautiful collages were created by a lady called Mary Delaney who lived in the eighteenth century. She was an expert needlewoman and made delicate collages using plant life as her theme. She did not start making her collages until she was seventy-two – a craft for all ages!

You may think that only paper is used in collage, but that is far from the truth. Twentieth century artist, Georges Braque, used very unusual materials in his work. He introduced imitation wood paper and fabric to his pictures. Perhaps some of the most unusual collages come from an artist called Kurt Schwitters, who made pictures using rubbish that he found in his city life, such as tickets, rags, advertisements and newspaper.

You don't have to be particularly artistic to create a collage. It really is a question of colour and balance. Pieces can be moved round and played with until you are satisfied with the arrangement, and then simply stuck down.

If, like me, you are a hoarder, then this book is definitely for you. I've always been drawn to brightly coloured pieces of fabric, coloured papers, ribbons, sequins and jewels. I must admit to having boxes of bits hidden here and there around my home. This book has given me the excuse to get all those boxes out. Felt, foil, feathers and foam; leaves, seeds and even plastic and polythene can be used for collage. The list is endless. A walk along a beach or in the countryside can provide you with a wealth of material to use. Alternatively just look around your own home and see what you can come up with.

So there you sit with your boxes of goodies. Perhaps the next question is what to make a picture of. As you work through this book, you will come across collages of butterflies, fish, aliens, spiders, flowers, fairies and even an Egyptian god. By the time you have completed all the projects in this book, you will have created a collage art gallery. Perhaps, more importantly, it will have inspired you to create your own collages using your interests, hobbies or even your favourite colour as a theme. Good luck with your sticking!

***Opposite**
This bright collage by H. Roger Rodgers
is called* Tree of Life.

Materials

Collage materials are inexpensive and easy to find. You will not need all the things listed here to begin your new hobby. In fact, you will be able to find a lot of materials in your own home. Keep a box for storing snippets of card and fabric that you think will come in handy for your projects.

Note Whenever you use glue or pens, you should cover your working area with newspaper. Wear old clothes and work on a tidy, flat surface. Have a damp cloth ready in case of spills.

PVA glue is used to stick card and fabric to a base board. Watered down, it is used to glue scrunched tissue paper to a surface. It dries hard and shiny. The **paste spreader** and **brushes** are used to apply glue.

Pieces of **thin card** are used to make templates, to cover with scrunched tissue paper and to cut into shapes.

It is best to use **thick card** as a base board for your collage as it does not warp when glued.

Scissors are used to cut thin card, paper, fabric, ribbon, cord and thin plastic. **Old scissors** are used to cut sandpaper.

Brightly coloured **felt** is ideal for collage work as it does not fray when cut. Shimmery **fabrics** can be used to create a more delicate look. **Chalk** is used to draw round a template on dark felt.

Crepe paper is cut into leaf and petal shapes. **Tissue paper** is scrunched and glued on to a base board to create a textured effect.

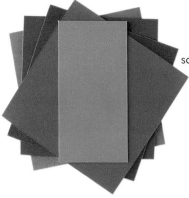

Coloured sheets of **high-density foam** are cut with scissors to make mosaic pieces.

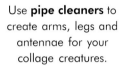

Use **pipe cleaners** to create arms, legs and antennae for your collage creatures.

Sequins, **sequin trim**, **plastic eyes**, **coloured gems**, **beads**, **red wool** and **green** and **silver cord** are all used for decoration. **Sticky tape** is used to attach wool at the back of a picture.

Use **newspaper** to protect your work surface. **Sandpaper** is used to create a textured background. **Textured wallpaper** is used to create a stone background.

Pompoms are used as the bodies of collage creatures. **Decorative floss** creates a smoky effect.

A **ruler** and **pencil** are used for measuring paper and card and for drawing straight lines. Embossing work is done with a **ballpoint pen**. A **run-out ballpoint pen** is ideal for scoring lines. A **permanent black felt tip pen** is for drawing on plastic and **compasses** are for drawing circles.

Handmade papers are used as a base when making natural-looking cards. **Skeleton leaves** are used for decoration.

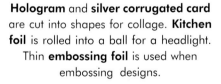

Hologram and **silver corrugated card** are cut into shapes for collage. **Kitchen foil** is rolled into a ball for a headlight. Thin **embossing foil** is used when embossing designs.

A **cardboard box lid** is decorated with **junk** items to create an unusual collage.

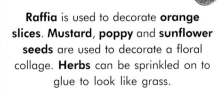

Raffia is used to decorate **orange slices**. **Mustard**, **poppy** and **sunflower seeds** are used to decorate a floral collage. **Herbs** can be sprinkled on to glue to look like grass.

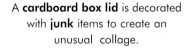

Sea Scene

A third of the surface of the world is covered by water. These seas and oceans are full of life. Most fish live in the upper part of the seas, down to a depth of 600m (2000 feet). Below this lurk strange deep-sea fish living in the darker waters. In this project we create the movement of water using layered and scrunched tissue paper. Our brightly coloured fish dives across the collage, its jewelled decorations catching the light.

YOU WILL NEED

A4 piece of thick card
Thin white card
Coloured tissue paper
Watered down PVA glue
Paste brushes
Scissors
Pencil
Coloured gems

1 Paste a section of your base board generously with some watered down PVA glue. Lay a piece of scrunched up tissue paper on to the glue and dab it with a paste brush until it lies flat, but with scrunched creases, as shown. Overlap the next piece of tissue paper slightly and continue in this way until the board is covered.

2 When the board is dry, use scissors to cut off the overhanging tissue paper.

3

Transfer the fish pattern on page 31 on to thin white card. Page 28 shows you how to transfer a pattern. Cut the fish shape out. Scrunch and glue pieces of tissue paper in a lighter colour over the surface of the card fish.

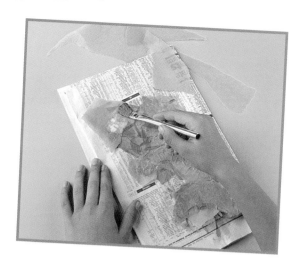

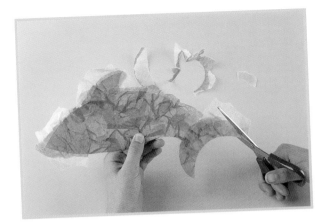

4 Use a different coloured tissue paper to cover the head, tails and fins. Scrunch and glue as before.

5 Tear circles of tissue paper and stick them on to the body section. Leave to dry. Cut off the overhanging tissue paper.

6

Glue the fish to the base board. Glue one coloured gem to each spot on the fish's body. Glue a gem in place for the fish's eye. You can glue a smaller gem on top to make a realistic pupil for the eye.

FURTHER IDEAS
Make a fish bowl filled with smaller fish made in the same way.

Butterflies

The beautiful colours of the butterfly inspired this collage. There are about one million known kinds of insect. A lot of them use their shape and colour either to attract a mate or to scare off an enemy. How many brightly coloured insects can you think of? Multicoloured sequins are the perfect decoration for our butterfly collage. The wings shimmer against the dark background, giving a real feeling of movement.

YOU WILL NEED

Dark-coloured thick card, 8 x 24cm (3 x 9½in)
Thin card for template
Thin coloured card
Coloured pipe cleaners
Coloured sequins
Pencil
Scissors
PVA glue

1 Make a template of the butterfly pattern on page 30. Page 28 shows you how to make a template. Draw round the template three times on thin coloured card. Cut out three butterflies.

2 To make the butterfly bodies and antennae, cut an 18cm (7in) length of coloured pipe cleaner for each butterfly. Bend them in half and curl the ends as shown. Glue one body down the centre of each butterfly.

3 Glue coloured sequins on to the card wings, overlapping them slightly so that the card is completely covered.

 Bend the wings upwards slightly either side of the body.

 Turn the butterflies over and run one line of glue down each body section.

6

Press the butterflies on to your dark-coloured thick card so that they overhang the edges of the card.

FURTHER IDEAS

Create a shimmering dragonfly using shiny fabric for the wings and beads and gems for the body.

Roman Mosaic

The Romans loved to decorate their large city villas. Though they were often quite plain on the outside, inside could be sumptuous. They used small pieces of coloured stone, called 'tesserae', to cover their floors, placing them so that they formed intricate patterns. These were called mosaics. This project shows you how to make a mosaic starfish collage using small pieces of coloured foam. Don 't worry if all the pieces are not exactly square – your collage will look more realistic if they are slightly irregular.

YOU WILL NEED

20cm² (8in²) square of thick black card
Three sheets of coloured foam
Thin card • Scissors
PVA glue • Pencil
Ruler

1 Use a pencil and ruler to draw a line 33mm (1¼in) from each edge of your thick card, to create a border.

2 Cut 1.5cm (½in) strips from two pieces of different coloured foam. Mark 1.5cm (½in) sections all along the strips, and cut them into squares.

3 Glue a row of foam squares around the edge of the black card, using alternating colours. Glue a second row of squares inside the first row as shown.

12

4 Photocopy the starfish design on page 29 on to thin card and cut it out to make a template. Place the starfish template on a coloured piece of foam and draw round it with a pencil. Cut it out.

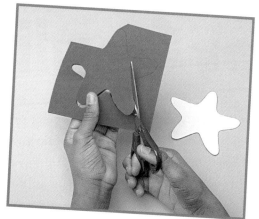

 Ask an adult to help you use the photocopier.

5 Draw wavy lines across the starfish with a pencil. Cut along the wavy lines. Arrange the cut pieces into a starfish again in the middle of your mosaic border.

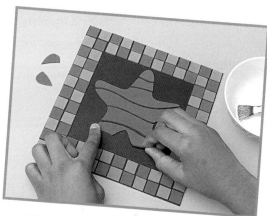

6 Glue the pieces down.

FURTHER IDEAS
Make a dolphin picture in a mosaic frame.

Creepy Crawlies

Some people are frightened of spiders, so this project could be a bit of a challenge! They are, however, fascinating creatures. Did you know that most spiders have eight eyes and that they taste through their feet? Some large spiders can live to twenty-five years and some South American varieties actually eat birds! What other amazing facts can you find out about spiders? These colourful pompom spiders with their pipe cleaner legs and wobbly eyes aren't quite so scary, so have fun creating this creepy crawly collage.

1 Cut out irregular paper stone shapes from wallpaper. Arrange them on your thick card base board to look like a stone wall. Some of the end 'stones' will have to be cut in half to fit. Glue them on to the base card and leave to dry.

2 Turn the base board over and tape a length of wool to the top right-hand corner. Wrap the wool round the card to create a fan-shaped web on the front. Tape the end of the wool to the back of the card to secure it.

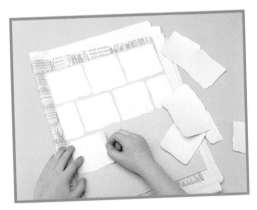

3 Wrap another length of wool across the bottom of the card in the same way, and tape the end at the back to secure it.

Cut two pipe cleaners in half. Tie the four pieces together in the middle with a piece of wool to make the legs of the spider.

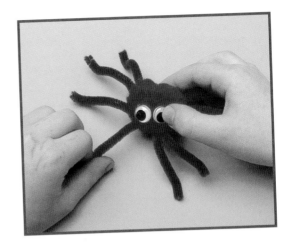

5 Bend the legs as shown. Glue a pompom body to the place where the legs meet. Glue two plastic eyes on to the pompom. Make three spiders in the same way.

6

Glue two spiders on to the stone wall and one in the centre of the web.

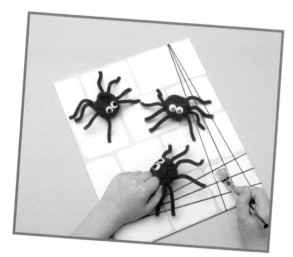

FURTHER IDEAS

Make centipedes from pompoms with snipped felt strips for legs, glued on to a background of paper leaves.

Sunflower Card

This project uses real sunflower seeds to decorate the centre of a paper sunflower. Sunflower seeds, and the seeds of other plants such as the poppy, are edible (unless you are allergic to nuts and seeds!) We grind seeds to spice our food, add them to our breads and cook with them. Oil can be extracted from certain seeds and, of course, seeds are also planted to grow a new crop. Try writing a list of different seeds and what we can do with them.

1 Score and fold the rectangle of thick card down the middle to make a greetings card (see page 28). Glue the square of lighter-coloured card to the middle of the front.

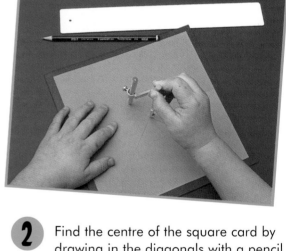

2 Find the centre of the square card by drawing in the diagonals with a pencil and ruler. Set your compasses to 3.5cm (1¼in) from the point to the pencil. Put the point in the centre of the square and draw a circle.

3

Take two 7 x 50cm (2¾ x 19¾in) strips of coloured crepe paper. Cut petal shapes along one long edge using the pattern on page 30 to help you.

4

Run a 1cm (½in) line of glue around the outside of the pencil circle. Press the straight edge of the petal strip round the circle, scrunching the paper to make it fit. Complete one circle.

5

Run another line of glue round the inside of the circle and press the second petal strip round it in the same way.

6

Spread the circle generously with glue, overlapping the base of the petals slightly. Press the sunflower seeds into the glue and leave to dry.

FURTHER IDEAS

Make a bright poppy in the same way, using poppy seeds for the flower centre.

Fairy Card

Every country has its own stories about mythical creatures. Fairies, elves, gnomes, goblins, pixies, leprechauns – how many different creatures can you come up with? Fairy tales have entertained children throughout the world for hundreds of years. These stories are often exciting, sometimes scary and frequently offer a moral at the end of the tale. This project uses shimmering fabric, glittery cord and sparkly gems and beads to create a magical fairy card.

YOU WILL NEED

Coloured card, 18 x 21cm
(7 x 8¼in)
Coloured felt
Shiny fabric • Silver cord
Small gems • Star sequins
Large glittery beads
PVA glue • Scissors
Pencil

1 Score and fold the coloured card lengthways to make a greetings card (see page 28). Transfer the face pattern on page 29 on to felt (also see page 28). Cut it out and glue it to the front of the card.

2 Glue two small gems to the face for eyes. Squeeze a blob of glue on to the top of the circle. Crumple some silver cord and press it into the glue to make hair.

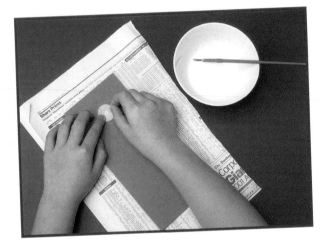

3 Make wing templates using the pattern on page 29. Draw round them on shiny fabric and cut them out. Squeeze some glue just below the head and press the ends of the wings into place.

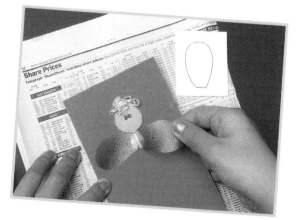

4

Cut a 12cm (4¾in) length of silver cord. Thread each end with a bead and knot to secure. Place the piece of cord across the wings and glue it in the middle. This will make the fairy's arms.

5

Cut a 30cm (11¾in) length of silver cord for the legs. Thread each end with a bead and knot as before. Fold the cord in half and glue the fold just under the arms.

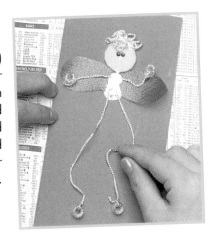

6

Use the pattern on page 29 to make a template of the dress shape, cut it out from felt and stick it onto the card just below the head. Glue a halo of star-shaped sequins around your fairy's head, and one sequin to the dress.

FURTHER IDEAS

Why not make a pixie to go with your fairy card? Put a feather in his cap.

Junk Truck

Everything in nature is recycled. Vegetation and animal remains feed the soil, which in its turn, nourishes new life. We can play our part by recycling rubbish that is not biodegradable, that is, it doesn't rot away. Nowadays there are factories that recycle paper, glass, aluminium cans, car tyres, some plastics, old clothes and lots more. You can create a collage using junk found around your home. Collect plastic, polythene and polystyrene packaging instead of putting it in the bin. Look for paper, string and bottle tops too – you will be amazed at how much junk you find.

YOU WILL NEED

Cardboard box lid
Junk: coloured plastic containers,
lids, polythene, string,
polystyrene, foam packing
and plastic netting
Kitchen foil
Permanent felt tip pen
PVA glue • Scissors

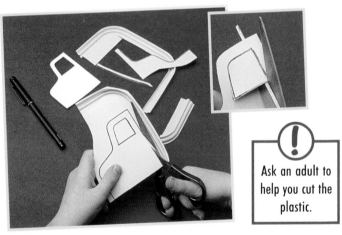

(!) Ask an adult to help you cut the plastic.

1 Make templates from the pattern on page 30, using the technique shown on page 28. Place the cab template on a piece of coloured plastic and draw round it with a permanent felt tip pen. Cut it out.

Note To cut the window hole, first cut across the upright bar at the back of the cab. This makes it easier to move the scissors, and will not show when you stick the cab down.

2 Cut a piece of coloured polythene slightly larger than the window hole. Glue it on to the back of the plastic so that it covers the hole.

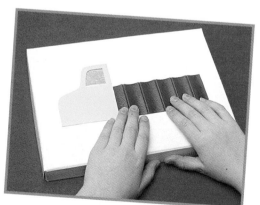

3 Glue the cab on to the box lid. Use a template as before to cut the back of the truck out of coloured plastic. Glue it behind the cab.

 4

Cut out three circles of black plastic for the wheels. Cut three smaller circles of foil and glue one to the middle of each wheel. Glue the wheels along the bottom of the truck.

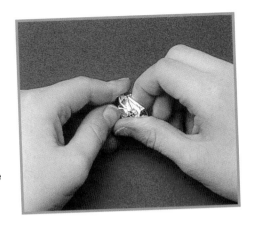

5 Roll a ball of foil and flatten it slightly for the headlight. Glue it into place.

6

Now fill your truck with junk! Cut your bits of junk into small pieces and glue them to the back of the truck.

FURTHER IDEAS

Make a junk robot from the plastic tray inside a box of chocolates.

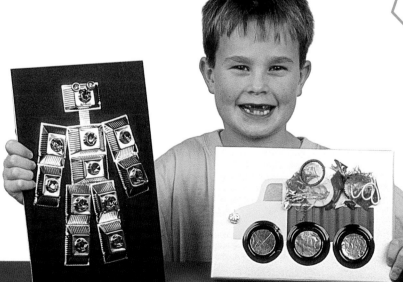

Egyptian God

The Ancient Egyptians believed in many gods. Some of the gods shown in their pictures looked half animal and half human. Anubis had the head of a jackal – a dog-like animal. The Egyptians believed that he was in charge of the underworld. Priests who prepared bodies for burial wore Anubis masks while performing their duties. In this collage, Anubis is shown wearing a sparkling headdress, and standing in front of some sandpaper pyramids.

YOU WILL NEED

Thick coloured card 25 x 23cm (10 x 9in)
Thin card • Black felt
Sheet of sandpaper
Gold sequin trim
Coloured gem
Scissors • Old scissors
PVA glue • Ruler
Chalk • Pencil

1 Glue a 15 x 23cm (6 x 9in) piece of sandpaper across the lower half of a 25 x 23cm (10 x 9in) piece of thick coloured card. Make pyramid templates as shown on page 28, using the patterns on page 31, and draw round them on the back of another piece of sandpaper. Cut out the pyramid shapes and glue them on the horizon line.

2 Make templates of the Anubis patterns. Lay them on black felt back to front, and draw round them with a piece of chalk. Cut out the felt shapes, cutting along the inside of the chalk lines.

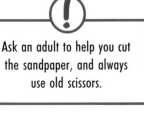

(!) Ask an adult to help you cut the sandpaper, and always use old scissors.

3 Spread the felt pieces with glue and then turn them over and stick them on to the sandpaper background.

4

Glue a coloured gem in place for the eye. Squeeze a line of glue down the left-hand and right-hand edges of the headdress shape. Press a length of sequin trim on to the glue.

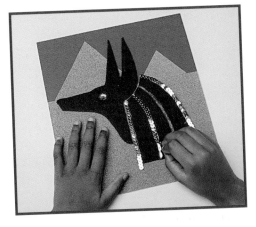

5

Use chalk to draw two curved lines between the sequined edges of the headdress. Squeeze glue down each line and glue lengths of sequin trim in place.

6

Trim the ends as shown. Glue a length of sequin trim along the top and bottom of the headdress. Leave to dry.

FURTHER IDEAS

Make a Chinese dragon using felt and fabric. What other animals can you think of that are connected to certain countries?

Leaf Card

Leaves and plants are very important to our planet. They take in carbon dioxide from the air and give off oxygen which we need to survive. Dried leaves and fruits provide us with beautiful shapes and textures which are ideal for collage work. Just look at the delicate skeleton leaf. You can see clearly the fine network of strands that kept the leaf supplied with water and nutrients. Use an earthy coloured card for this project, as it will really set off these natural forms.

1 Cut an 18 x 9.5cm (7 x 3¾in) rectangle of thin coloured card. Score and fold it down the middle, as shown on page 28. Measure and cut a 9 x 9.5cm (3½ x 3¾in) rectangle of handmade paper.

2 Tear a small strip from each edge of the handmade paper, to give it a rough-edged look. Glue the rectangle to the front of your card.

3 Put the skeleton leaf on a piece of scrap paper and spread it carefully with a little glue. Press it gently on to the front of your card and leave to dry.

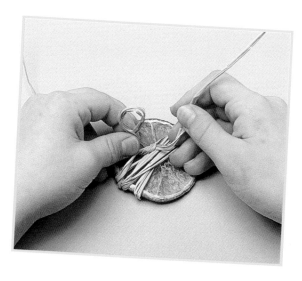

 4

Wrap a dried orange slice with raffia and tie it in a bow at the front. Trim the ends of the raffia using scissors.

 5 Glue the wrapped orange slice to the card at the base of the leaf.

 6

Cut two 2.5cm (1in) squares of coloured card and glue them to your leaf card: one to the top right and one to the bottom left.

FURTHER IDEAS

Make a tree with a raffia trunk, paper leaves and card and mustard seed oranges. Add grass made from dried herbs sprinkled over wet glue.

Alien

The Earth is a small planet in a huge universe. The universe is made up of countless planets and stars. Nobody knows how big the universe is or if it has any limits. Do you think there is life on other planets? If you think there is, what do you think these alien life forms would look like? In this project, metal foil is used to create the alien. Backed with colourful planets drifting in a dark sky, this collage is definitely out of this world!

YOU WILL NEED

Coloured thick card
Coloured tissue paper
Thin white card
Thin silver embossing foil
Pipe cleaners • Sticky tape
Coloured and silver sequins
Watered down PVA glue
Paste brush • Ballpoint pen
Pencil • Plate • Cup
Scissors • Newspaper

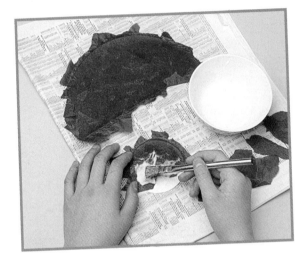

1 Draw round a plate and cup to make a circle and a semicircle on a piece of thin white card. Cut out the shapes. Glue torn pieces of tissue paper over the card shapes and leave to dry.

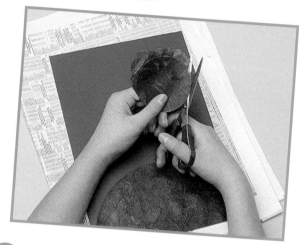

2 Cut off the overhanging tissue paper. Glue the large semicircle to the bottom of a 20 x 30cm (8 x 11¾in) piece of coloured card. Glue the smaller circle to the top right-hand corner.

3

Ask an adult to help you use the photocopier.

Photocopy the alien pattern on to paper. Cut round the pattern, leaving space around the edges as shown. Place a piece of embossing foil slightly larger than the pattern on a folded newspaper. Lay the pattern on top and tape it to the foil. Use a ballpoint pen to trace the design through on to the foil. Press firmly.

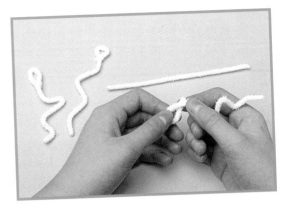

4

Remove the pattern and cut out the alien head and body from the foil. Turn them over. Glue them on to the planet card.

5

Bend four pipe cleaners into zigzags. Bend one end of each pipe cleaner into a circle to make hands and feet. Twist to secure.

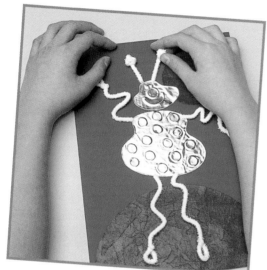

6

Glue the pipe cleaner arms and legs into position. Cut two 10cm (4in) lengths of pipe cleaner to make antennae. Roll one end of each length into a ball. Glue the antennae on to the top of the alien's head. Decorate with sequins.

FURTHER IDEAS
Make a rocket collage using silver card, hologram card and sequins. Use decorative floss for the rocket's fiery trail.

Techniques

Making a greetings card

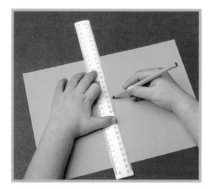

1 Measure halfway across your card and mark the halfway points at the top and bottom.

2 Using a ballpoint pen that has run out of ink, and a ruler, score a line down the card between the marks.

3 Fold the card along the scored line to make a nice sharp crease.

> (!) Ask an adult to help you to photocopy the patterns.

Transferring a pattern

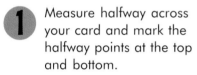

1 Photocopy the pattern on to thin white card. You can enlarge it on the photocopier if you need to. You can use the photocopy for your project, or you can cut out the pattern to make a template.

2 Draw round your template to make the shapes you need for your collage projects.

28

Patterns

Pattern for the Roman Mosaic featured on pages 12–13

Pattern for the Alien collage featured on pages 26–27

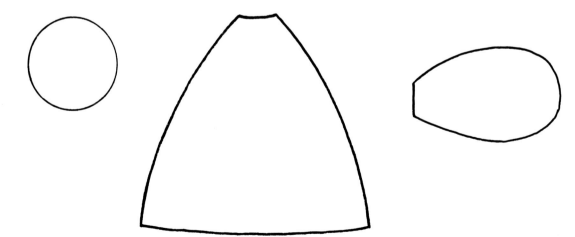

Patterns for the face, dress and wings for the Fairy Card featured on pages 18–19

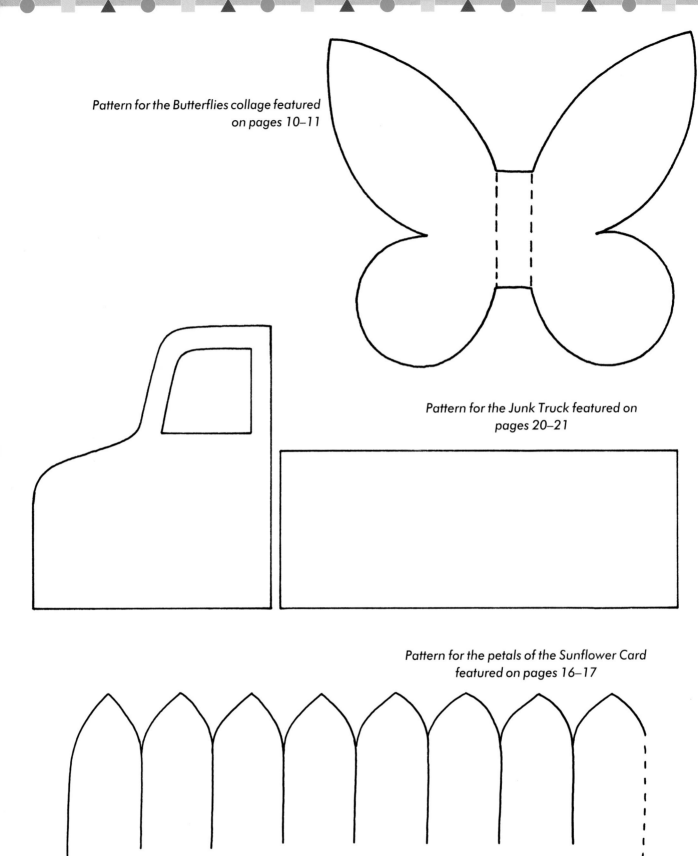

Pattern for the Butterflies collage featured on pages 10–11

Pattern for the Junk Truck featured on pages 20–21

Pattern for the petals of the Sunflower Card featured on pages 16–17

*The fish pattern for the Sea Scene
featured on pages 8–9*

*Pattern for the Egyptian God and pyramids
featured on pages 22–23*

Index

aliens 4, 26–27, 29

Anubis 22–23

beads 7, 11, 18, 19

Braque, Georges 4

brush 6, 8

butterflies 4, 10–11, 30

card 4, 6, 7, 8, 10, 11, 12, 13, 14, 16, 18, 22, 24, 25, 27, 28, 30

chalk 6, 22, 23

compasses 7, 16

crepe paper 6, 16

cord 6, 7, 18, 19

decorative floss 7, 27

Delaney, Mary 4

Egyptian god 4, 22–23, 31

embossing foil 7, 26

fabric 4, 6, 11, 18, 23

fairies 4, 18–19, 29

feathers 4, 19

felt 4, 6, 15, 18, 22, 23

felt tip pen 7, 20

fish 4, 8–9, 31

foam 4, 7, 12, 13

foil 4, 7, 20, 21, 26

gems 7, 8, 9, 11, 18, 22, 23

greetings card 16, 18, 28

handmade papers 7, 24

hologram card 7, 27

junk 7, 20–21, 30

leaves 4, 6, 15, 24–25

Matisse 4

mosaic 7, 12–13

paper 4, 7, 15, 20

paste spreader 6, 16

pipe cleaners 7, 10, 14, 15, 26, 27

plastic 4, 6, 7, 20, 21

plastic eyes 7, 14, 15

pompoms 7, 14, 15

PVA glue 6, 8, 10, 12, 14, 16, 18, 20, 22, 24, 26

raffia 7, 24, 25

ribbons 4, 6

Romans 12, 29

rubbish 4, 20

ruler 7, 12, 16, 22, 28

sandpaper 6, 22

Schwitters, Kurt 4, 5

scissors 6, 7, 8, 10, 12, 14, 16, 18, 20, 22, 24, 25, 26

scoring 7, 16, 18, 24, 28

scrunch 6, 8, 9, 17

seeds 4, 7, 16, 17, 25

sequins 4, 7, 10, 18, 19, 26, 27

sequin trim 6, 22, 23

spiders 4, 14–15

starfish 12–13

sticky tape 6, 14, 26

sunflower 7, 16–17, 30

tissue paper 6, 8, 9

transferring 8, 18

truck 20–21, 30

wallpaper 7, 14